Junior's Colors

by Phil Vischer

Thomas Nelson, Inc.
Nashville

Art Direction:
Ron Eddy

Lead 3D Illustrator:
Aaron Hartline

3D Illustrators:
Thomas Danen, Robert Ellis,
Joe McFadden, Joe Sapulich
and Nathan Tungseth

Render Management:
Jennifer Combs and Ken Greene

Published in Nashville, Tennessee, by Tommy Nelson™,
a division of Thomas Nelson, Inc.

Jell-O® is a registered trademark of
Kraft Foods, International, Northfield, IL.

Library of Congress Cataloging-in-Publication Data
Vischer, Phil.
    Junior's Colors / by Phil Vischer.
         p. cm.
    Summary: Bob the Tomato and Larry the Cucumber teach the
different colors using common objects and rhyme.
    ISBN 0-8499-1487-6
    1. Colors — Juvenile literature. [1. Color.] I. Title.
QC495.5.V57 1997
535.6 — dc21

                       97-23985
                       CIP
                       AC

Printed in the United States of America

99 00 01 02 03 BVG 9 8

Dear Parent

We believe that children are a gift from God and that helping them learn and grow is nothing less than a divine privilege.

With that in mind, we hope these "Veggiecational" books provide years of rocking chair fun as they teach your kids fundamental concepts about the world God made.

– **Phil Vischer**
President
Big Idea Productions

Junior Asparagus loves to draw.
He knows all his colors, too!

Here are some pictures
of things that he saw —
He wanted to share them with you!

White is the color of big fluffy clouds
That float through the sky overhead.

WHITE

A marshmallow's white,
    and a big snowball fight,

But Bob is
    very red.

ORANGE

Orange is the color
of Laura the Carrot
And Lenny and Jimmy Gourd, too.

Yellow is mellow.
It's great for your Jell-O!
Or maybe the fur on a cat —

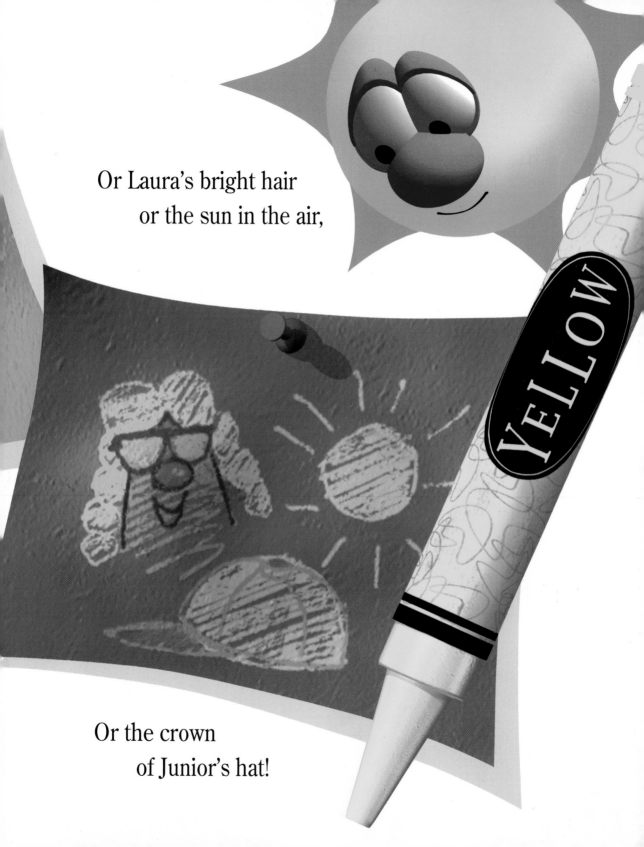

When Junior gets dirty
and needs a good scrub,
The water is
sparkling **Blue**.

So is the boat he
can float in his tub.

And the bottle that
holds his shampoo!

Black is the color
of nighttime —

When Junior is
tucked in bed.

A bowling ball's black,
    and a licorice snack,

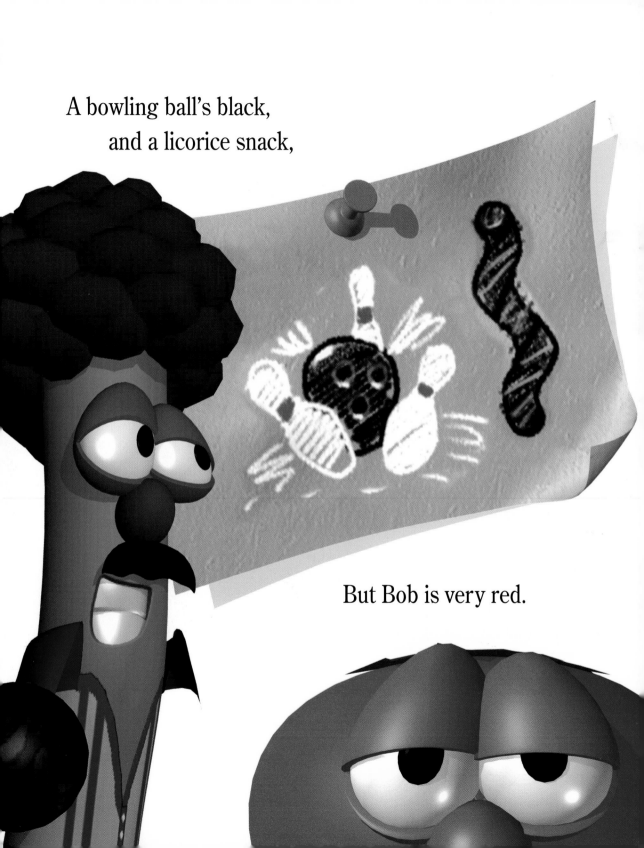

But Bob is very red.

Junior finds **Purple** on
lilacs and orchids,
The flowers his Mom
likes the most!

It's also in use
in his favorite juice

And the jelly
he puts
on his toast.

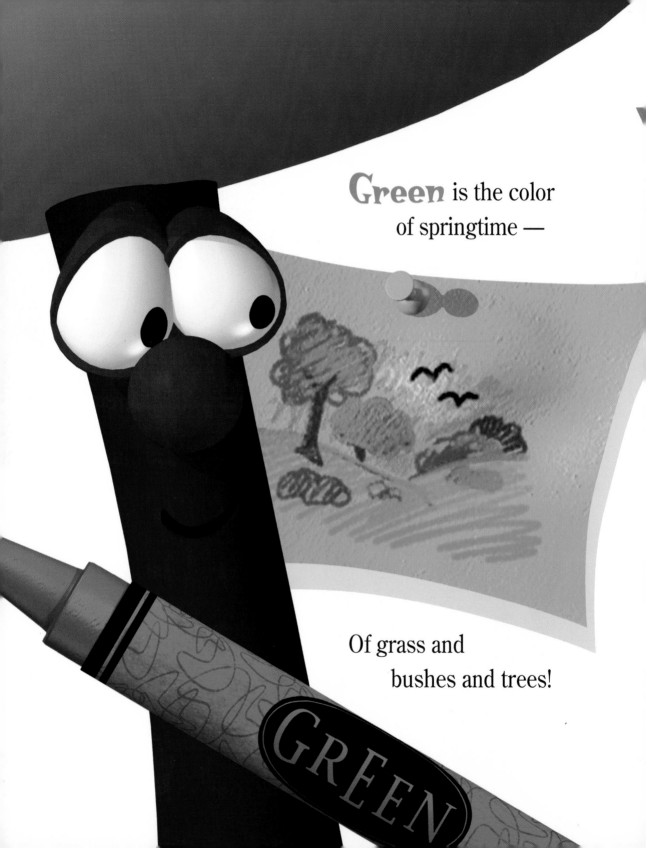

Green is the color
of springtime —

Of grass and
bushes and trees!

That's why if you fall
when you're
chasing a ball
You get green on your
elbows and knees!

When God made the world,
    he used all sorts of colors —
Some of them brighter
    and some of them duller.

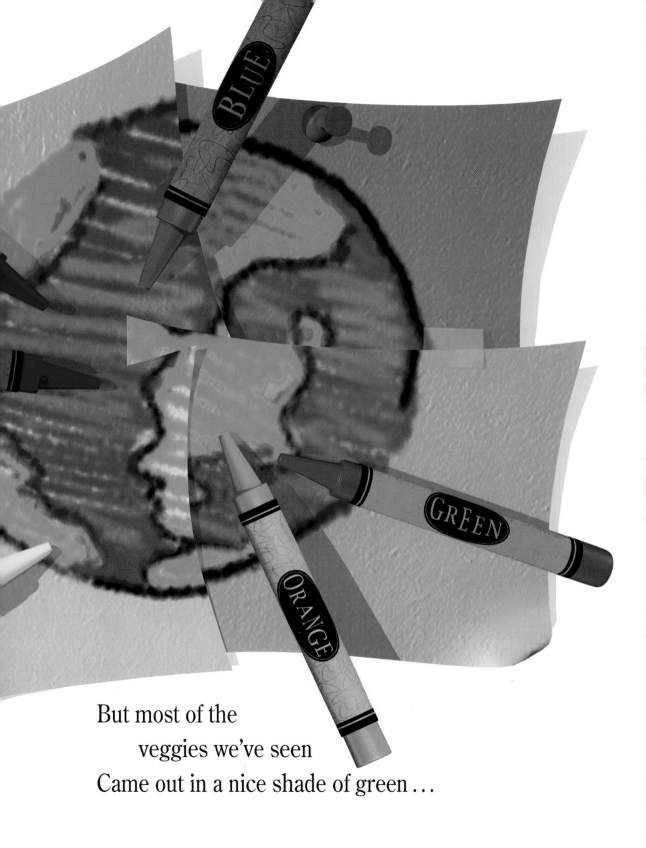

But most of the
  veggies we've seen
Came out in a nice shade of green …

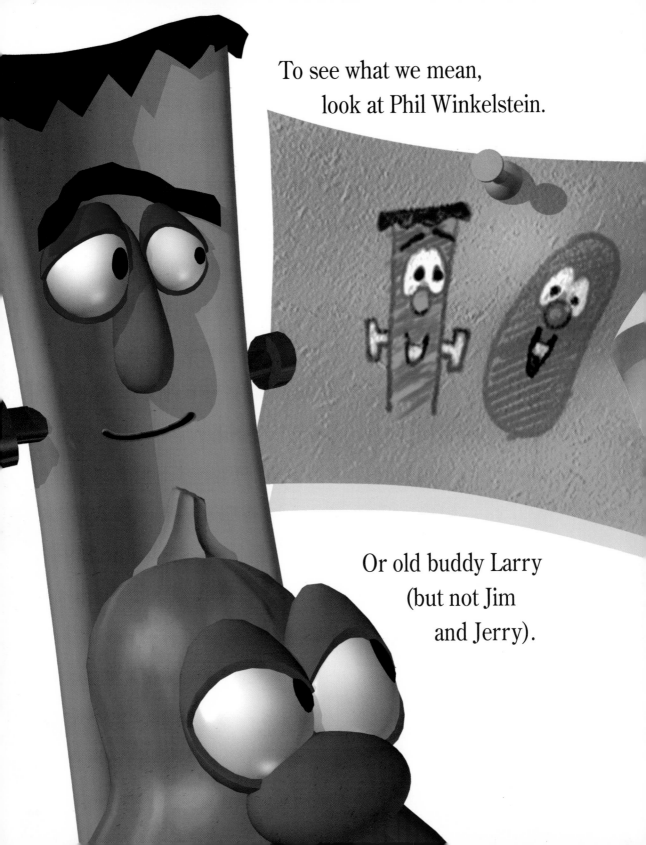

To see what we mean,
    look at Phil Winkelstein.

Or old buddy Larry
    (but not Jim
    and Jerry).

How 'bout Junior's mother?
Or Percy Pea's brother?

The scallions
(all three)
and Archie,
you see,

Are green
from toe
to head…

But Bob is very **Red**!